COCKROACHES

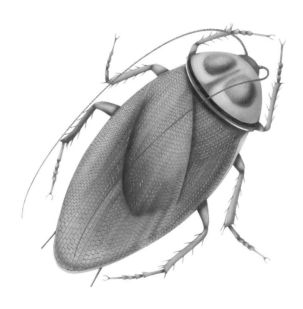

For a free color catalog describing Gareth Stevens' list of high-quality books and multimedia programs, call 1-800-542-2595 (USA) or 1-800-461-9120 (Canada). Gareth Stevens Publishing's Fax: (414) 225-0377.
See our catalog, too, on the World Wide Web: http://gsinc.com

Library of Congress Cataloging-in-Publication Data

Green, Tamara, 1945-
    Cockroaches / by Tamara Green ; illustrated by Tony Gibbons.
      p. cm. -- (The New creepy crawly collection)
    Includes bibliographical references and index.
    Summary: Examines the anatomy, behavior, and dangers of cockroaches, as well as ways of coping with them.
    ISBN 0-8368-1912-8 (lib. bdg.)
    1. Cockroaches--Juvenile literature. 2. Household pests--Juvenile literature.
[1. Cockroaches.] I. Gibbons, Tony, ill. II. Title. III. Series.
QL505.5.G74 1997
595.7'28--dc21   97-7342

This North American edition first published in 1997 by
Gareth Stevens Publishing
1555 North RiverCenter Drive, Suite 201
Milwaukee, Wisconsin 53212 USA

This U.S. edition © 1997 by Gareth Stevens, Inc. Created with original © 1996 by Quartz Editorial Services, 112 Station Road, Edgware HA8 7AQ U.K.

Consultant: Matthew Robertson, Senior Keeper, Bristol Zoo, Bristol, England.

Printed in Mexico

1 2 3 4 5 6 7 8 9 01 00 99 98 97

THE NEW
CREEPY CRAWLY
COLLECTION

COCKROACHES

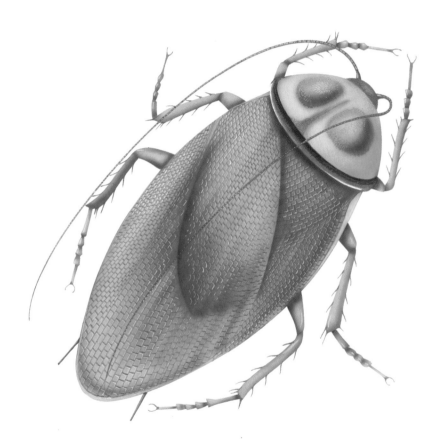

by Tamara Green
Illustrated by Tony Gibbons

Gareth Stevens Publishing
MILWAUKEE

Contents

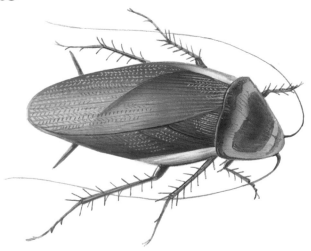

Getting to know cockroaches

"Yuk!" said the health inspector, as he noticed a shiny creature scrambling across the restaurant's kitchen floor.

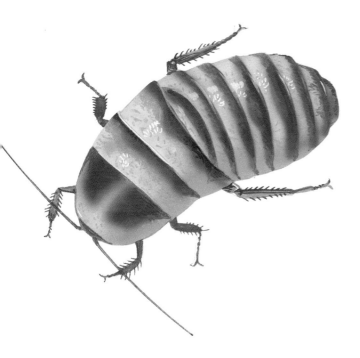

It was a cockroach, and it was after tiny scraps of food that should have been swept up earlier. The inspector would now report the restaurant to the authorities. Workers would have to be more careful about cleanliness in the future.

To most people, cockroaches suggest dirty surroundings. But do these insects actually carry disease? Should we be afraid of them? If they do get into our homes, how can we get rid of them?

As you turn the pages of this fascinating book, you'll find many enlarged illustrations of what are possibly the most disgusting of all insects. Strangely, though, some people have actually kept them as pets. Read on and find out whether *you*, too, could ever learn to love a cockroach!

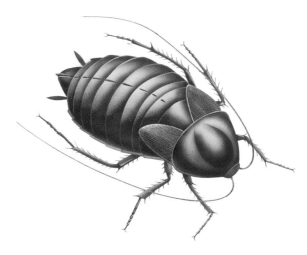

Nasty

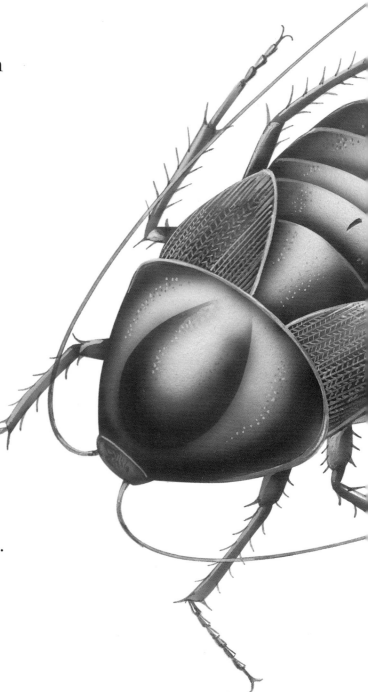

Most people are revolted by cockroaches. Even if you've never seen one in real life before, you'll easily recognize these pests. They vary a little in size, but the common cockroach — also known as the "black beetle" — is about 1 inch (2.5 centimeters) long.

You'll know them at once by the two very long, thin, jointed antennae on their heads. These seem to be constantly quivering. Although cockroaches have good eyesight, the antennae help them feel around for things and are also used for sniffing for scraps. And they have what looks like another, much shorter pair of antennae at the other end of their bodies.

A cockroach's six legs are long and spiky. It's no wonder they are such fast runners. That is why it is always hard to catch them. Notice, too, how their flat bodies are covered by what seems to be a sort of leathery shield.

pests

The most common cockroaches include the black beetle; the German cockroach, which is about 0.4 inch (1 centimeter) long, striped, and yellow-brown in color; and the American cockroach, which is about 1.2 inches (3 cm) long and is a reddish-brown color.

Some species of cockroaches do not have wings, while others have two pairs of tiny flaps for wings. In some species, the wings are more fully developed, but they still hardly ever fly and prefer life on the ground. You will rarely see a cockroach in flight.

A cockroach's head is often hidden under the thorax or middle part of its body. If you could look at one under a microscope, you would see that this greedy creature's mouth-parts are ideal for chewing.

Nightmare in the kitchen

Air conditioning and ventilation ducts, cracks in the walls or in baseboards, and the underside of flooring — all are likely hiding places for cockroaches by day.

They sometimes lurk there in large numbers. Then, at night, they venture out.

Cockroaches do not carry any specific diseases, but they can contaminate food with germs. So if you smell a strange odor in the kitchen at breakfast, it might be only the garlic from last night's dinner. Hopefully, it is not from a colony of cockroaches that has paid a visit to your home. You can sometimes tell they have been around because of the bad smell they leave behind as a calling card.

Whether at home, in a hotel, or at a restaurant, anyone who is in charge of a kitchen and unlucky enough to be visited by these pests is in for a nasty experience.

9

Outdoor life

As you already know, cockroaches sometimes infest kitchens. But they are not only house-dwellers. Some also thrive in the open air. You can sometimes find them under piles of rotting leaves and other decaying vegetation, or under dead bark. But you will need to look carefully because they will probably be well camouflaged.

Cockroaches are also nocturnal, so you would probably have a better chance of seeing them crawling around when it is dark. But don't go out on your own at night to look for them. Instead, ask an adult member of your family to take you out on a cockroach safari at dusk — if he or she is not too disgusted by the thought of them!

If you use a flashlight, as in this illustration, you might be able to spot some because they are attracted to artificial light.

Some of the cockroaches that prefer the outdoor life use their wings and occasionally fly around at night. But this usually happens only in tropical regions.

The outdoor cockroach's main menu consists of rotting leaves, dead insects, fungi, fruit that has fallen from trees or bushes, and wood. They are greedy and have enormous appetites for their size!

You'll probably notice, too, that the cockroaches' long antennae seem to quiver all the time and that they run very fast.

Even if you are tempted to take some cockroaches home to observe them close-up, you had better not do so. They might be females that can lay eggs, and your home would soon become thoroughly infested with these little creatures — a scary thought!

Greedy scavengers

Cockroaches love the environment of a messy or dirty kitchen, as we have seen. But this is not just because there is more chance of finding food there than anywhere else in your house or apartment.

These insects originate from tropical parts of the world. Although millions of generations may have lived in cooler areas for centuries, they still instinctively seek out warmth.

Amazingly, though, cockroaches are attracted not only to leftovers and crumbs of food but will also eat paper and fabric of all kinds, including leather. In fact, they have been known to chew their way through book bindings; and strange as it may seem, they like shoe polish and ink, too.

So watch out for your jacket, sneakers, and jeans, as well as any leftover food if cockroaches have been spotted running around in your house!

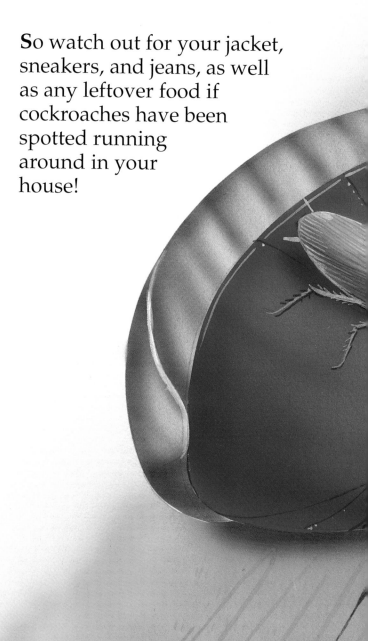

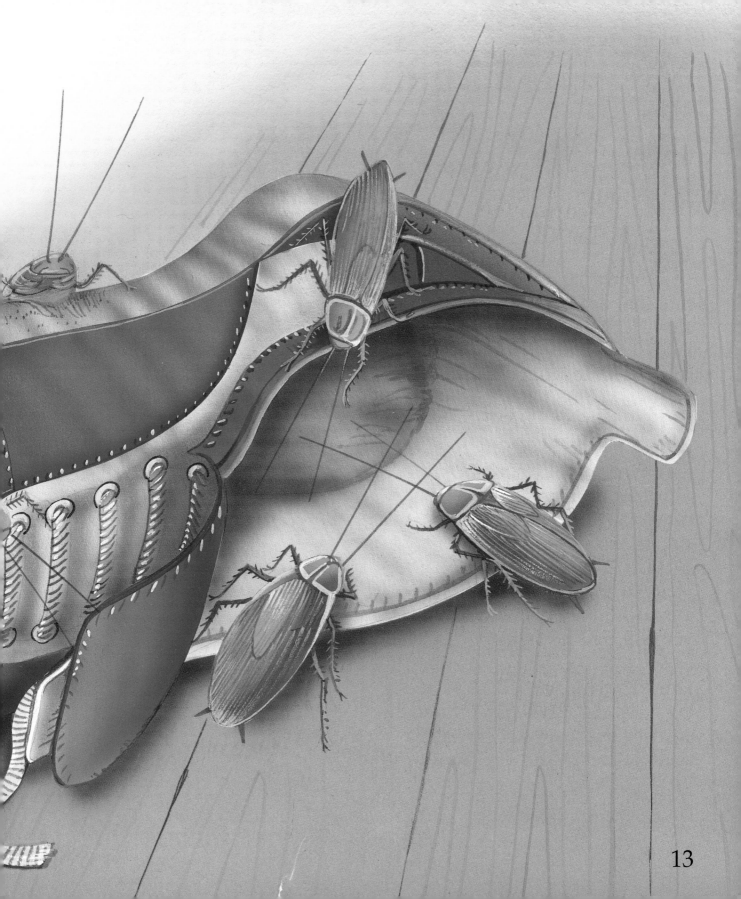

Infested cargo

Insects sometimes reach distant places by accident. They creep into the cargo holds of ships, like stowaways, and soon they are in an entirely different country.

This was probably the case with the cockroach. Lots of these insects were brought to England by the famous sailor Sir Francis Drake. This highly respected sixteenth-century seaman not only circumnavigated the world but also led England's war against the Spanish Armada. He even became a pirate, taking booty from many Spanish trading vessels.

One such ship carried sacks of exotic spices. Drake later found swarms of dreaded cockroaches in these sacks.

Could many of the cockroaches now alive in various areas of the world possibly be direct descendants of the cockroaches that once crawled around in Drake's booty or in similar cargo on its way to foreign ports?

Abandoned

Look at this German cockroach. It must be a female. You can tell because it seems to be carrying a brown "purse" attached to the back of its body. Of course it is not a real purse with money inside!

A cockroach's ootheca usually has two rows of eggs, with eight in each. These sixteen eggs will hatch about eight weeks later. But some types of cockroaches have an ootheca that contains more than twice as many eggs.

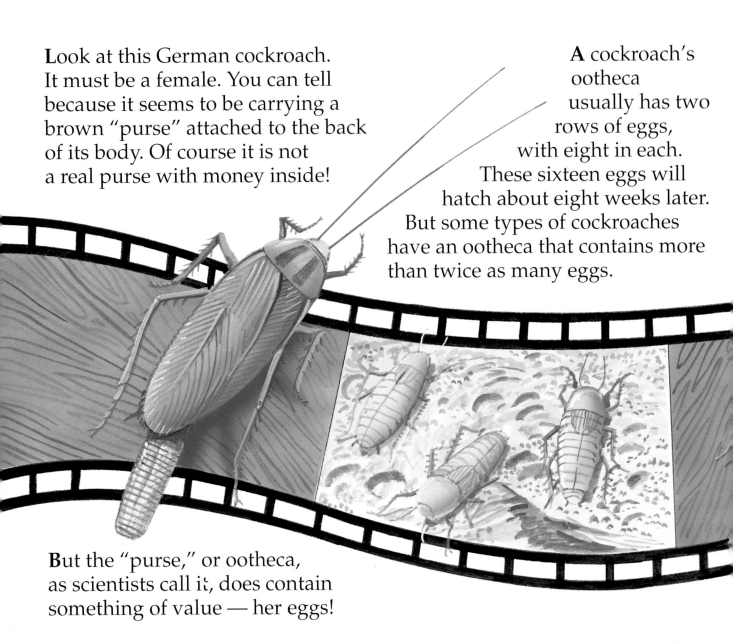

But the "purse," or ootheca, as scientists call it, does contain something of value — her eggs!

A day or so later, she will deposit her ootheca in a crevice or crack. Then she will abandon it.

If there are lots of eggs, the mother carries the ootheca until just before the eggs hatch.

16

babies

The mother cockroach now takes no further interest in her family. She does not nurse them or bring them up.

The babies are this active right away because they must take care of themselves.

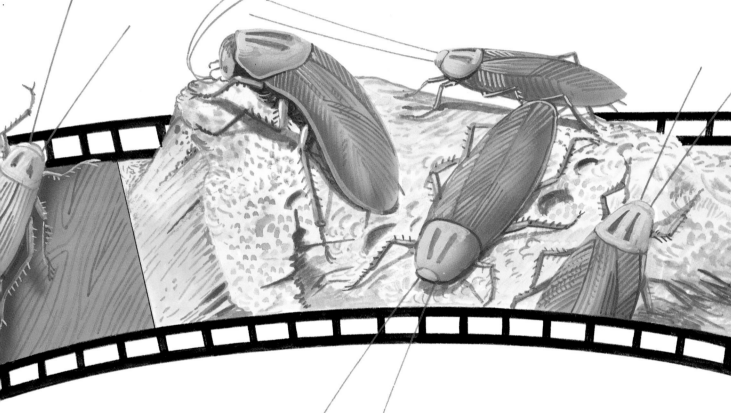

Instead, the baby cockroaches have to fend for themselves. They are white at first and immediately start running here and there when they emerge.

While still growing, the babies shed their skin several times and darken. It is easy to see how quickly a cockroach colony can grow, if the mothers lay at least sixteen eggs at a time!

17

Coping with

You now know that there's nothing cockroaches like more than a dirty kitchen. That's why it is so important to keep your home clean and free from crumbs and scraps. Cover and store all food very carefully. You also need to keep your trash cans clean and regularly disinfected. Cockroaches will actually dirty more than they consume, and serious food poisoning can result if a cockroach has crawled over a plate or dish. If you suspect this, throw the food away. It can be helpful to use an insecticide, if you know where the pests hide. But only an adult should ever use an insecticide powder or spray because these can be poisonous and may irritate the skin. If cockroaches become a real problem in your kitchen or

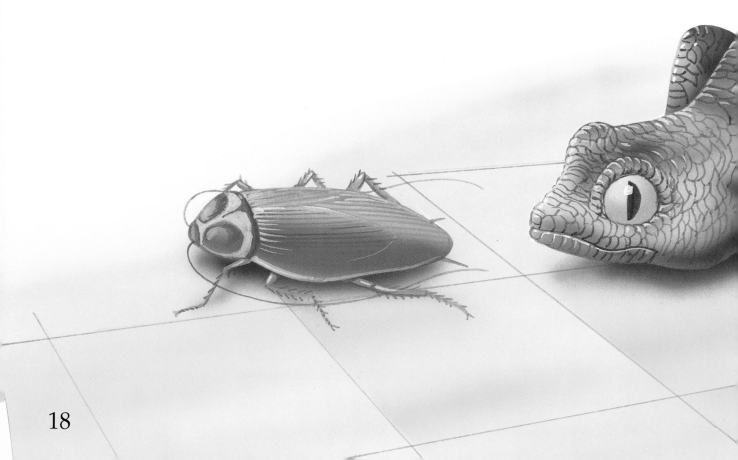

cockroaches

elsewhere, it is best to call in an environmental health officer or a pest control company. Meanwhile, you could simply swat or stomp on a cockroach, and then carefully throw it away. Make sure you wash your hands thoroughly afterward. And what about other methods of getting rid of them?

In the United States, some people with cockroaches in their homes have even started to keep geckos as pets. Geckos are tropical lizards that sleep by day but come out at night and hunt cockroaches. What a clever way of coping with these nasty pests!

A close relative

Cockroaches are hardly cute! However, they have a relative that is much more charming in appearance — the praying mantis. Study the illustration of an orchid mantis shown here, and you will soon understand how this insect got its name. As you can see, it is standing on only four of its six legs.

Its front legs, meanwhile, are held out as if it is praying. Don't be fooled! It is not doing anything nearly so harmless. A hungry predator, the praying mantis waits patiently to grab at passing prey, and it does so with lightning speed. The mantis is strictly a carnivore and will never eat vegetation, even though often surrounded by it, as you can see here.

Some mantises are green in color and are perfectly camouflaged among new leaves. Others are a pinkish color and are well hidden among blossoms or flowers.

The Indian mantis, however, is a shade of brown; it looks like the dead foliage on a forest floor and is practically invisible there.

Such camouflage helps disguise each type of mantis so that it will not be spotted easily either by its prey or its enemies. Native to warmer parts of the world only, most mantises can fly, but they do not often use their wings. If you try to catch and handle one, it may bite you. But do not worry; it is not venomous.

Did you know?

How long have cockroaches been around on Earth?

Paleontologists have discovered fossils of cockroaches that date as far back as 300 million years; the fossilized insects look just like the cockroaches of today. They probably ate scraps that dinosaurs such as Tyrannosaurus rex, which roamed our planet about 80 million years ago, left after their meals.

Can cockroaches ever be useful?

Japanese scientists have recently developed remote-controlled cockroaches by grafting microchips onto their backs. Equipped with mini-cameras, these tiny bionic creatures may become spies of the future! They might be sent in to photograph secret documents, for example — unless, of course, they are spotted and stepped on before they have a chance to complete their mission.

▼ Is the praying mantis a scavenger, like the cockroach?

They may be related, but the mantis and the cockroach are very different in their eating habits. While the cockroach likes scraps of all kinds, a praying mantis, *below*, only eats a creature it has killed itself. It then picks at it very delicately, like a well-mannered person, and takes only very small mouthfuls.

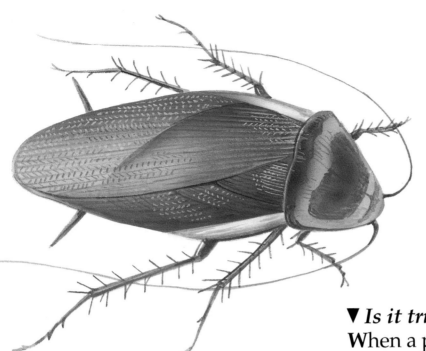

Are cockroaches cannibalistic?
Cockroaches will eat the dead of their own kind if kept in captivity, but they do not actually kill them for food. Instead, they wait until they have died naturally or been killed by another creature.

▼ *Is it true that cockroaches hiss?*
When a predator approaches, the hissing cockroach of Madagascar, off the eastern African coast, will expel air noisily in an attempt to frighten the enemy off. You can see this clever little creature *below*.

▲ *Is it true that cockroaches are sometimes specially bred?*
Some cockroaches are bred in zoos and universities so researchers can learn more about them. A few, such as the giant Australian cockroach shown *above*, are rare and bred in captivity in case they become extinct in the wild.

Does the female praying mantis lay her eggs in an ootheca, as the cockroach does?
The mother praying mantis also puts her eggs in this "purse" and deposits it on a plant or twig. It usually contains more eggs than a cockroach's ootheca, however.

Glossary

antennae — movable sensory organs, or feelers, on the head of an insect that are used for touching and smelling.

camouflage — markings or coloring that help an animal or plant disguise itself and blend in with its natural environment.

carnivore — a meat-eater.

insecticides — poisonous chemicals used to kill insects.

nocturnal — active at night.

paleontologists — scientists who study the remains of plants and animals that lived millions of years ago.

predators — animals that hunt and kill other animals for food.

prey — animals that are killed for food by other animals.

quiver — to shake or tremble.

scavengers — animals that eat dead or decaying matter.

species — animals or plants that are closely related and often similar in behavior or appearance. Members of the same species can breed together.

thorax — an insect's middle section, or chest cavity, which holds the heart and lungs.

Books and Videos

Cockroaches. Mona Kerby (Watts)

Cockroaches. Lynn Stone (Rourke)

I Can Read About Creepy Crawly Creatures. (Troll Communications)

Incredible Insects. (National Wildlife Federation)

Insect Mouthparts. (Encyclopedia Britannica Educational Corporation video)

Insects. (AIMS Media video)

The Insects. (Educational Images Ltd. video)

Index